Alfred's Basic Piano Library

Popular Hits • Level 6

Piano

T0011865

Arranged by Tom Gerou

This series offers Broadway, pop, and movie music arrangements to be used as supplementary pieces for students. Soon after beginning piano study, students can play attractive versions of favorite classics, as well as the best-known popular music of today.

This book is correlated page-by-page with Lesson Book 6 of *Alfred's Basic Piano Library*; pieces should be assigned based on the instructions in the upper-right corner of the title page of each piece in *Popular Hits.* Since the melodies and rhythms of popular music do not always lend themselves to precise grading, you may find that these pieces are sometimes a little longer and more difficult than the corresponding pages in the Lesson Book. The teacher's judgment is the most important factor in deciding when to assign each arrangement.

When the books in the *Popular Hits* series are assigned in conjunction with the Lesson Books, these appealing pieces reinforce new concepts as they are introduced. In addition, the motivation the music provides could not be better. The emotional satisfaction that students receive from mastering each song increases their enthusiasm to begin the next one.

27 Years Later (from *IT Chapter Two*). 5

Aerith's Theme (from *Final Fantasy VII: Advent Children*). 2

Ashokan Farewell (from the PBS series *The Civil War*) 15

Happy Together (The Turtles) 12

Havana (Camila Cabello) 20

I'll Be There for You (Theme from *Friends*). 31

Little Shop of Horrors (from *Little Shop of Horrors*). 28

Money (Pink Floyd) 18

Salamander Eyes (from *Fantastic Beasts: The Crimes of Grindelwald*) 22

Shallow (from *A Star Is Born*) 34

Speechless (from Walt Disney's 2019 *Aladdin*). 8

Star Wars® (Main Title) 25

Produced by
Alfred Music
P.O. Box 10003
Van Nuys, CA 91410-0003

alfred.com

ISBN-10: 1-4706-4273-5
ISBN-13: 978-1-4706-4273-0

Cover Photos: Music speakers: © Shutterstock.com / Martin M303 • Headphones: © Shutterstock.com / Jiri Hera

Use after pages 10–11.

Aerith's Theme

(from *Final Fantasy VII: Advent Children*)

By Nobuo Uematsu

Arr. by Tom Gerou

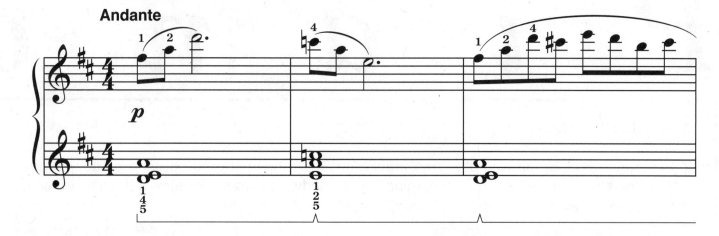

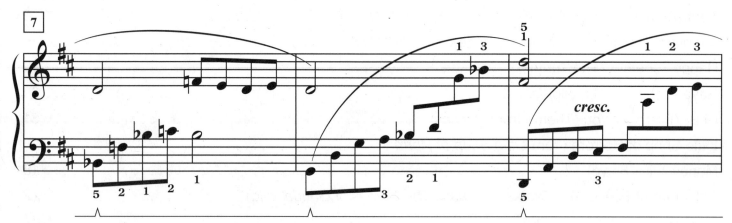

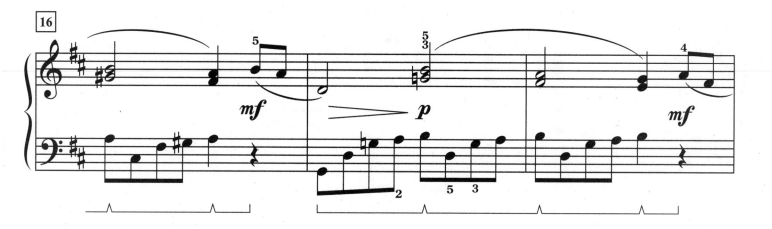

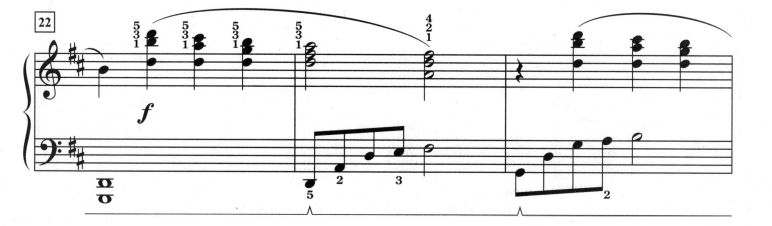

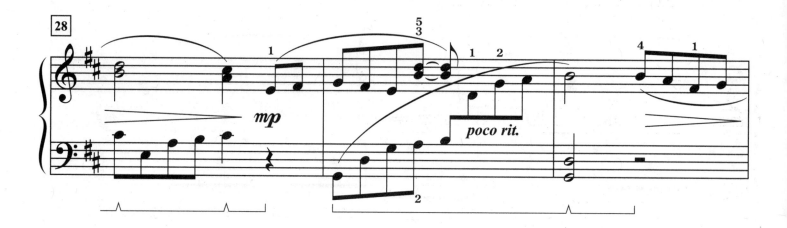

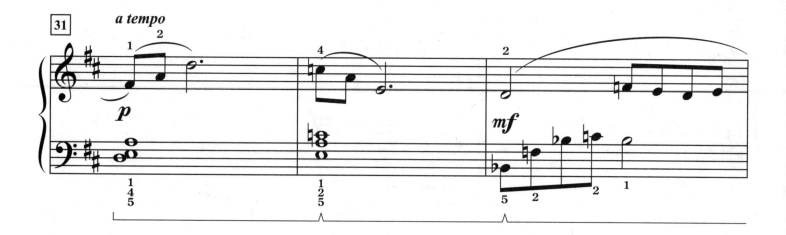

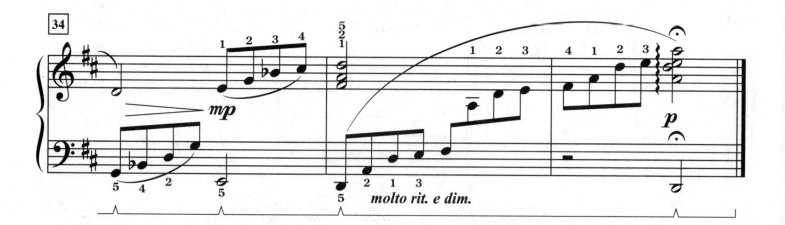

Use after pages 14–15.

27 Years Later

(from *IT Chapter Two*)

Composed by Benjamin Wallfisch
Arr. by Tom Gerou

Andante, with rubato

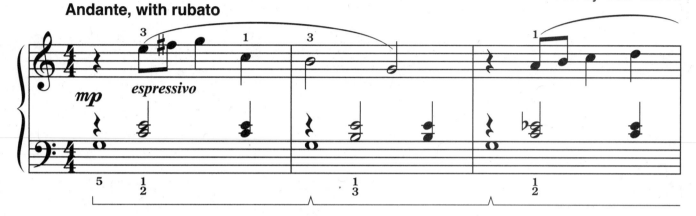

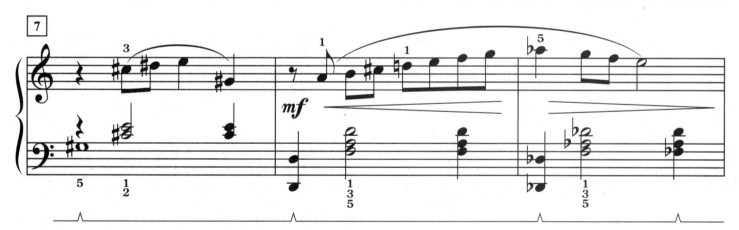

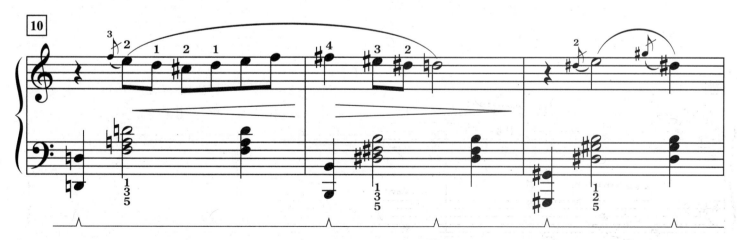

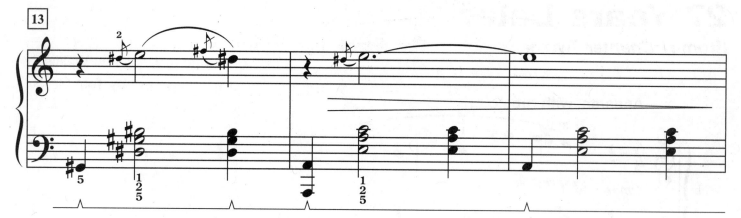

Use after pages 16–18.

Speechless
(from Walt Disney's 2019 *Aladdin*)

Music by Alan Menken
Lyrics by Benj Pasek and Justin Paul
Arr. by Tom Gerou

Moderately slow

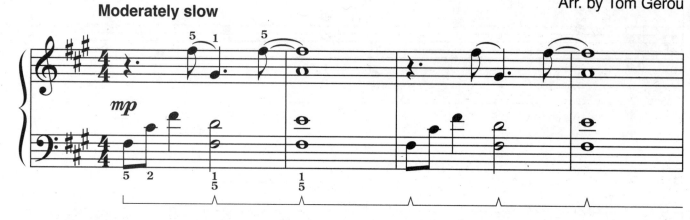

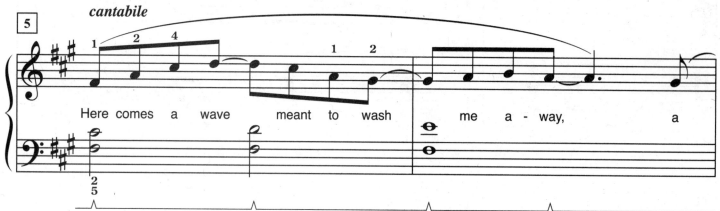

Here comes a wave meant to wash me a - way, a

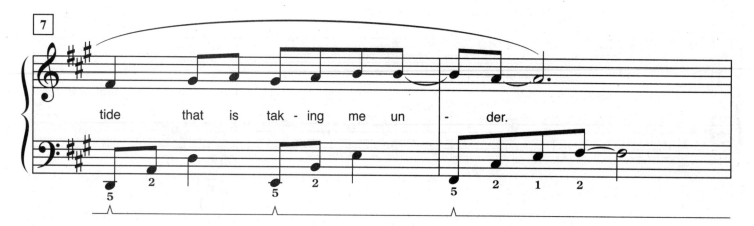

tide that is tak - ing me un - der.

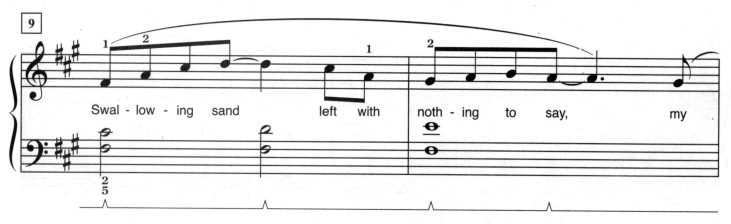

Swal - low - ing sand left with noth - ing to say, my

voice drowned out   in the   thun - der.   But I won't cry,

and   I won't   start   to   crum - ble,

when-ev - er they try   to   shut me   or cut me   down.

I   won't   be

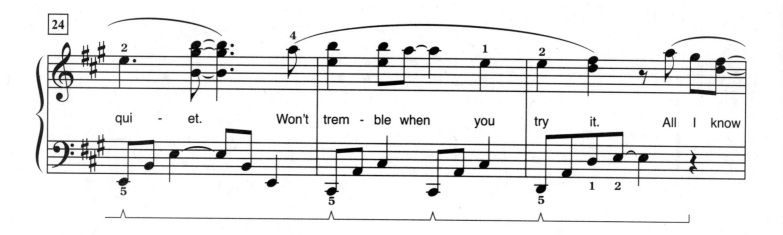

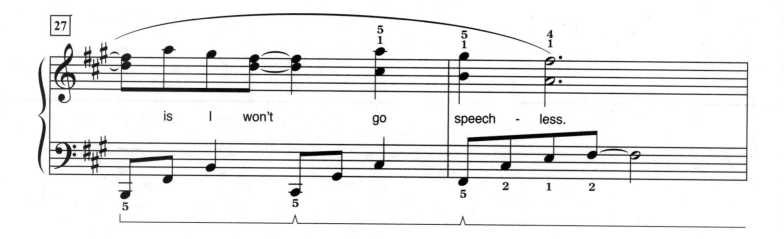

cate   me.   Don't you   un - der - es - ti -

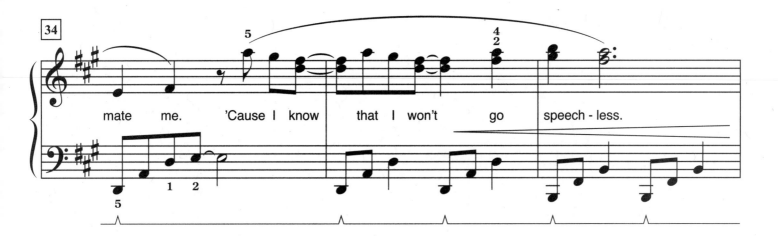

mate   me.   'Cause I know   that   I won't   go   speech - less.

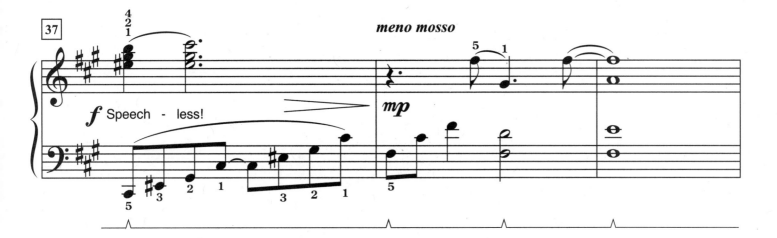

meno mosso

f Speech - less!   *mp*

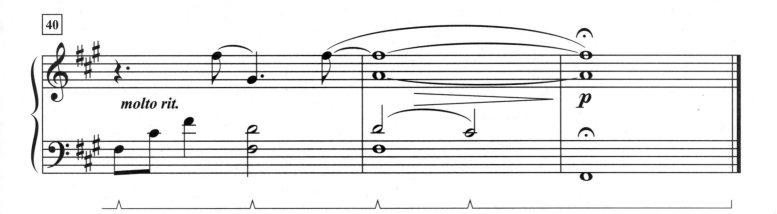

molto rit.   *p*

Happy Together

Use after pages 20–21.

Words and Music by
Gary Bonner and Alan Gordon
Arr. by Tom Gerou

Moderate swing tempo*

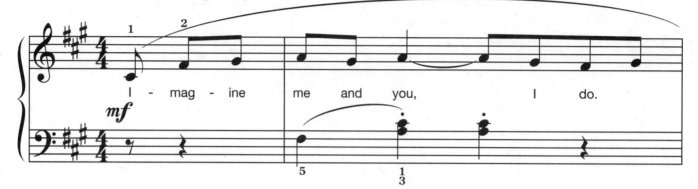

*Play the pairs of eighth notes a bit unevenly, long-short.

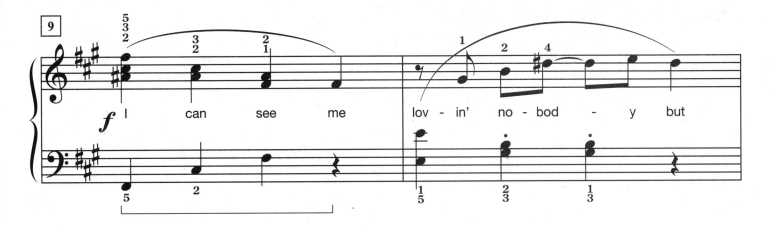

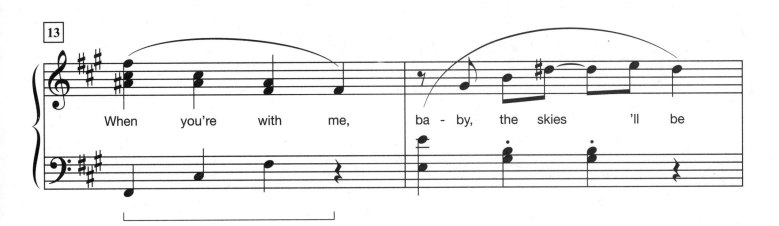

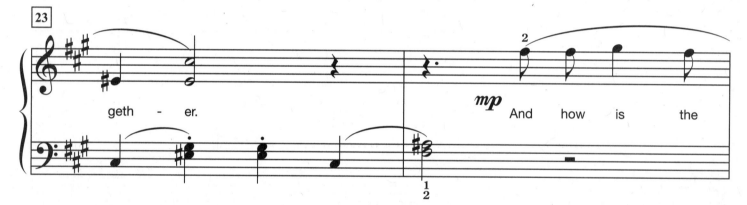

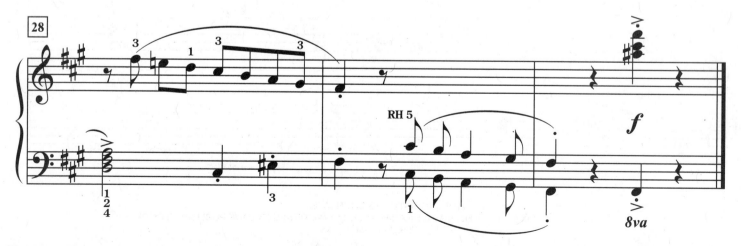

Ashokan Farewell
(from the PBS series *The Civil War*)

By Jay Ungar
Arr. by Tom Gerou

Moderato espressivo

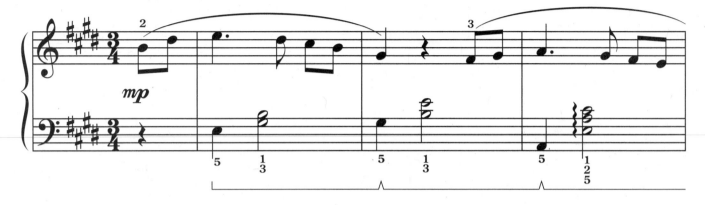

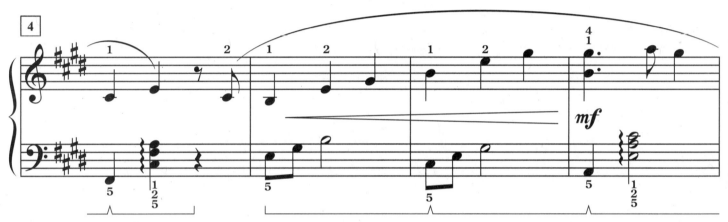

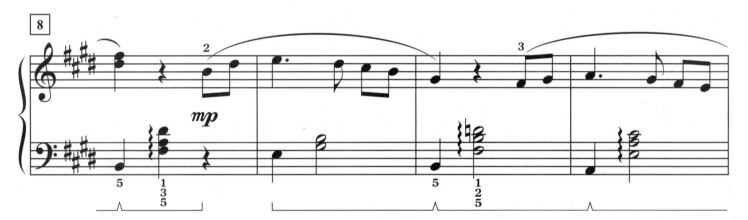

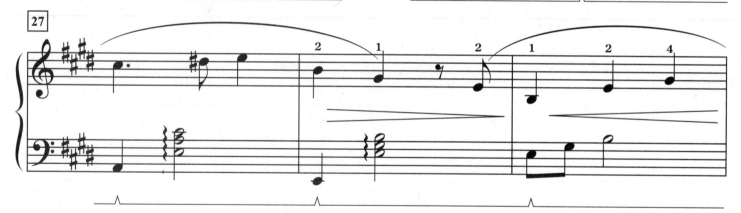

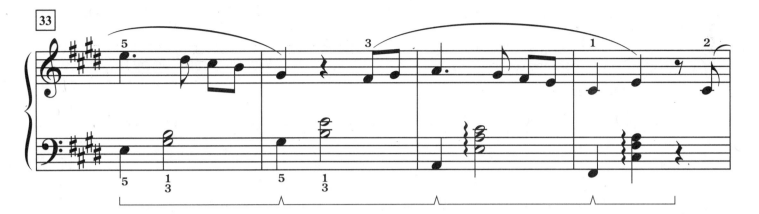

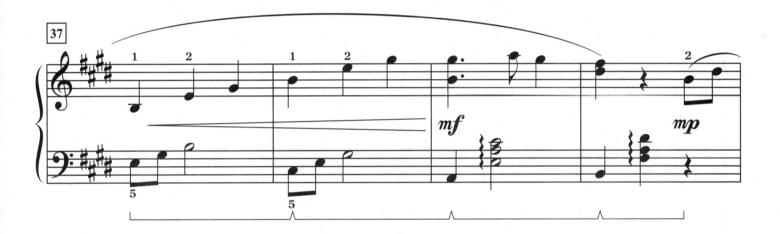

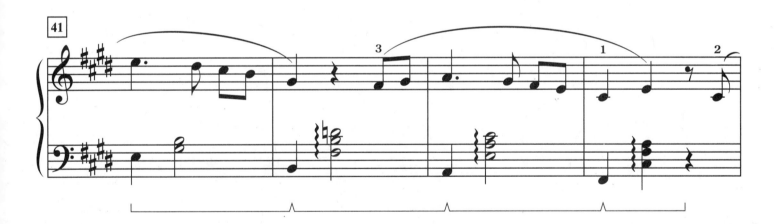

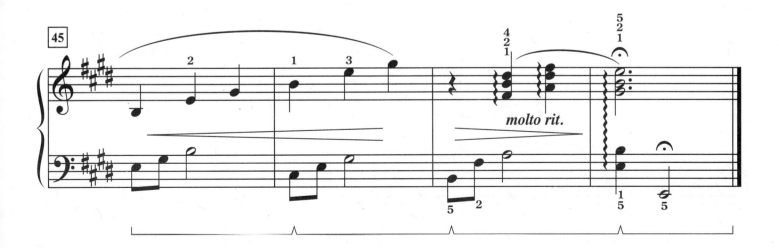

Money

7 means 7 beats to each measure.
4 a QUARTER NOTE ♩ gets one count.

Use after pages 32–33.

Words and Music by Roger Waters
Arr. by Tom Gerou

Moderate blues tempo

New car, cav - i - ar,   four - star   day - dream.
But if   you   ask   for a   raise,   it's   no   sur -

Think I'll buy   me   a   foot - ball team.
prise that they're giv - ing   none   a - way,

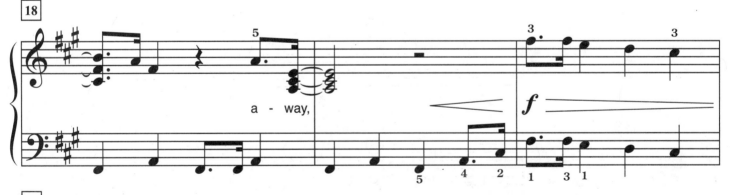

a - way,   a - way,

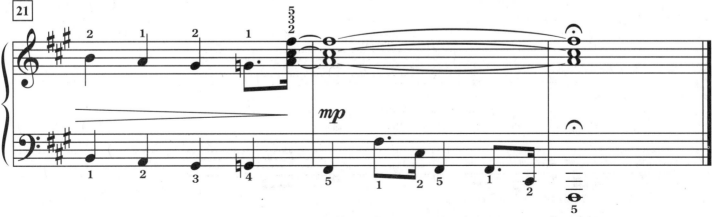

a - way,

Use after pages 34–35.

Havana

Words and Music by Brian Lee, Young Thug,
Louis Bell, Camila Cabello, Frank Dukes, Brittany Hazzard,
Ali Tamposi, Andrew Watt and Pharrell Williams
Arr. by Tom Gerou

Moderate Latin beat

Salamander Eyes
(from *Fantastic Beasts: The Crimes of Grindelwald*)

Use after pages 36–37.

Composed by James Newton Howard
Arr. by Tom Gerou

Tenderly, with expression

Moderately

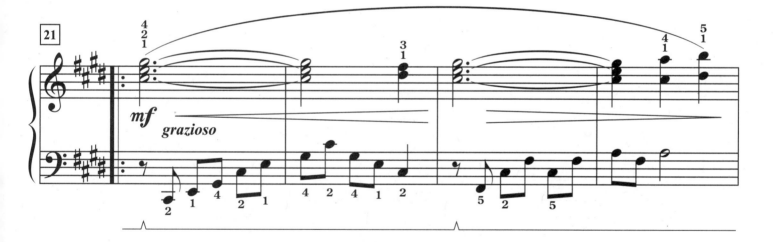

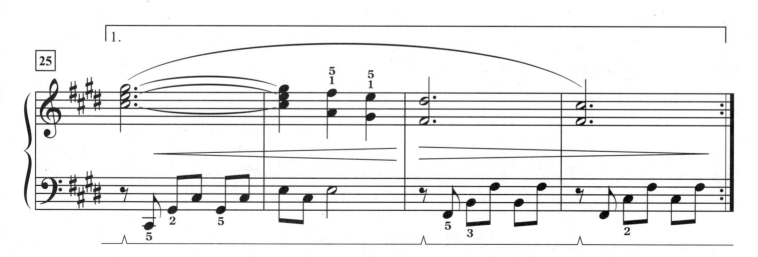

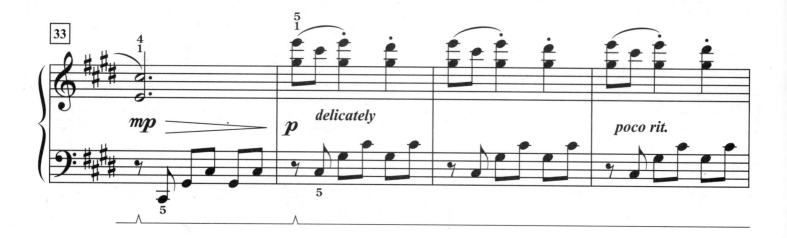

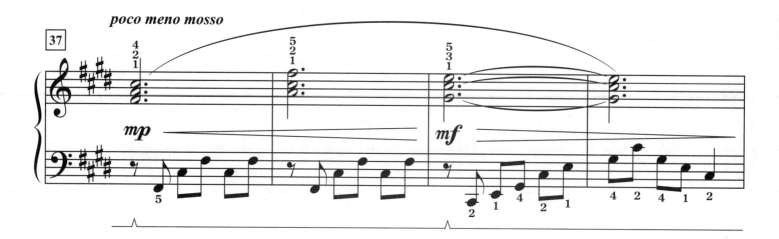

Star Wars
(Main Title)

By **JOHN WILLIAMS**
Arr. by Tom Gerou

Majestically, steady march

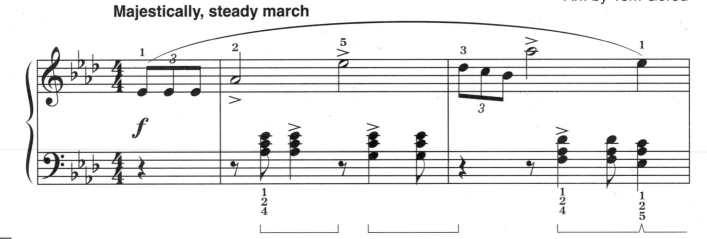

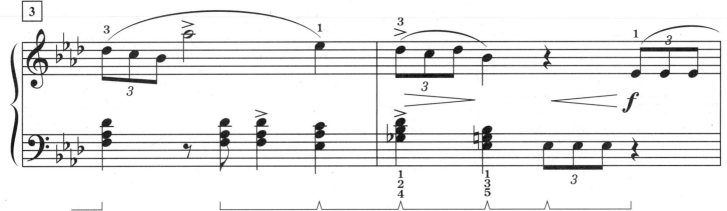

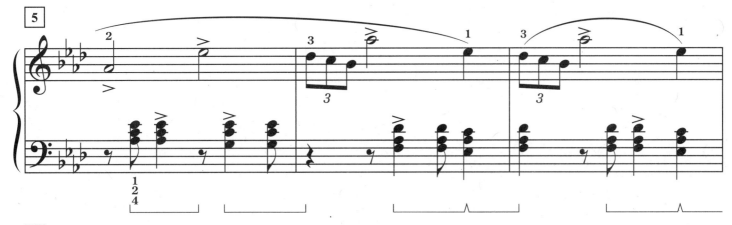

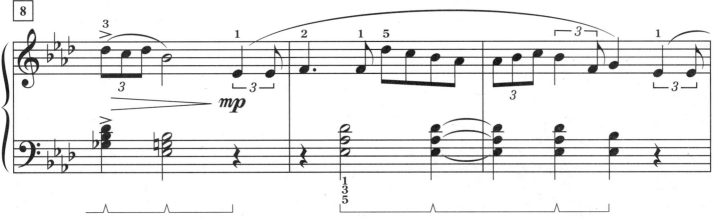

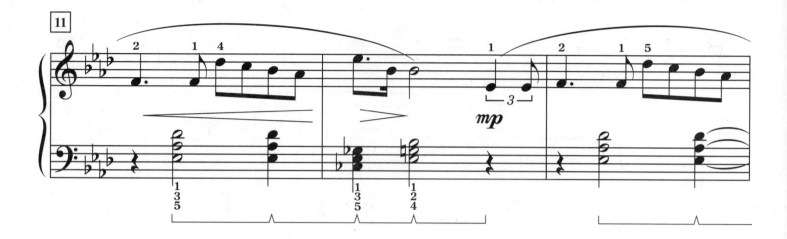

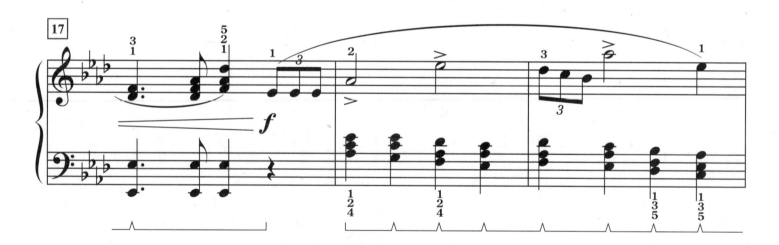

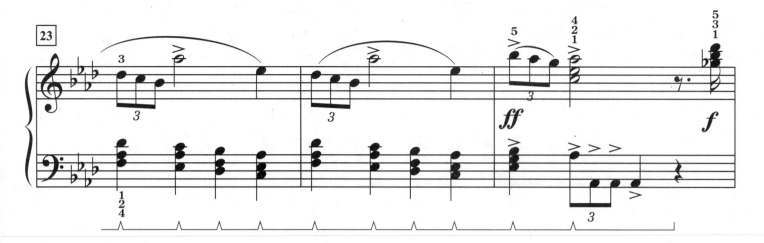

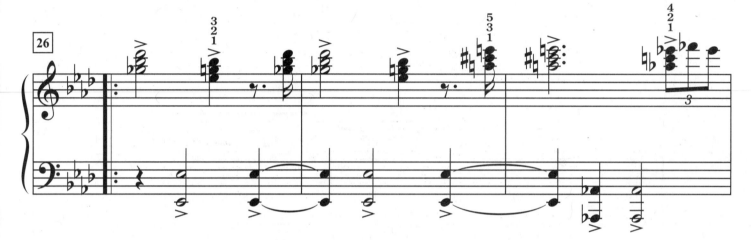

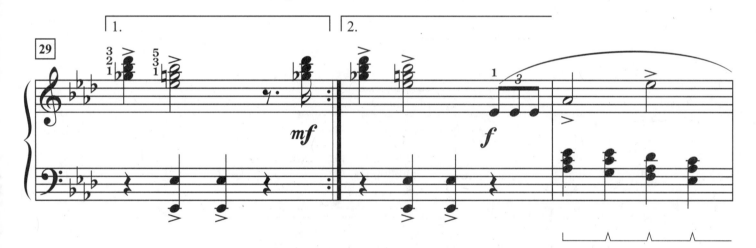

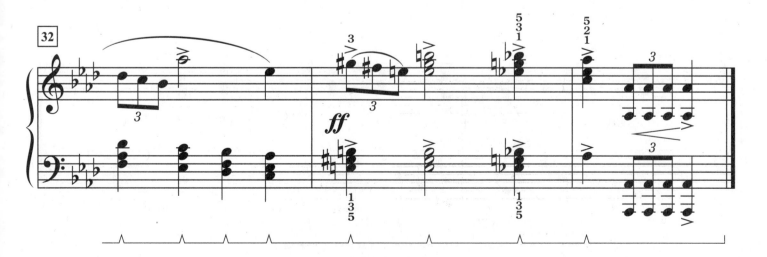

Little Shop of Horrors

(from *Little Shop of Horrors*)

Use after pages 43–45.

Words by Howard Ashman
Music by Alan Menken
Arr. by Tom Gerou

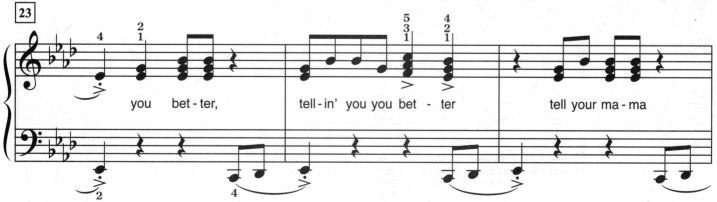

26 some-thin's gon-na get her. She bet - ter, ev - 'ry-bod - y bet - ter be-ware.

29

33 *f* Lit - tle shop, lit - tle shop-pa hor - rors. Bop - sh' - bop, you'll

36 nev - er stop the ter - ror. Lit - tle shop, lit - tle shop-pa hor - rors.

39 No, oh, oh, no, oh, oh, no, oh, oh, no!

I'll Be There for You

(Theme from *Friends*)

Words by David Crane, Marta Kauffman,
Allee Willis, Phil Solem and Danny Wilde
Music by Michael Skloff
Arr. by Tom Gerou

Fast rock

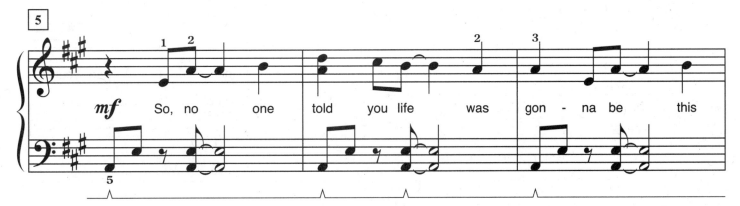

So, no one told you life was gon - na be this

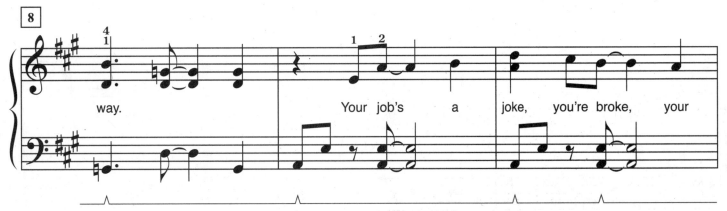

way.   Your job's a joke, you're broke, your

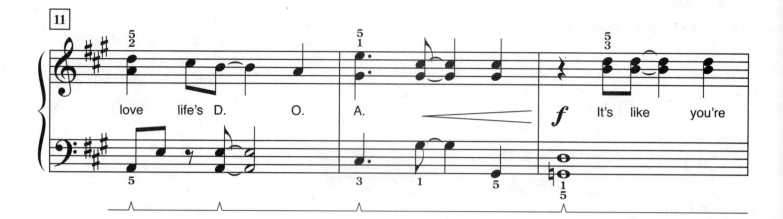

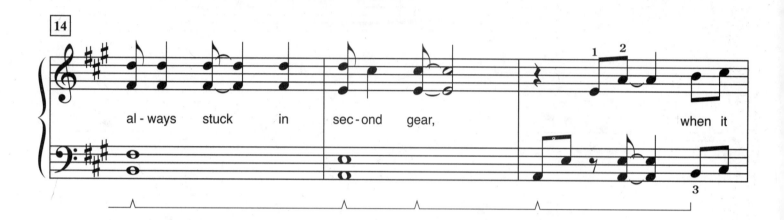

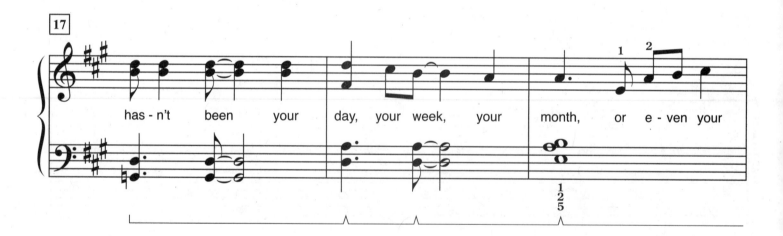

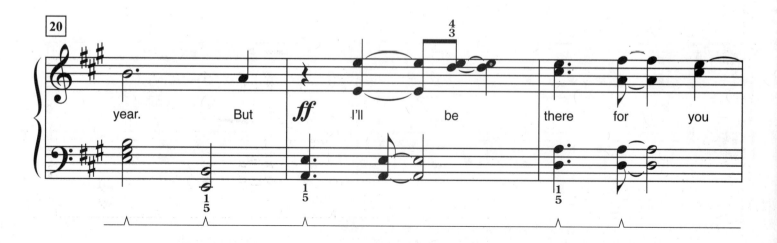

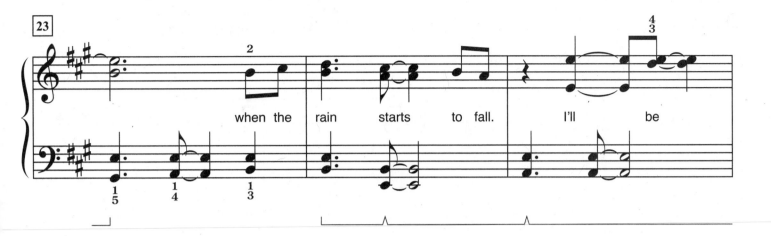

when the rain starts to fall. I'll be

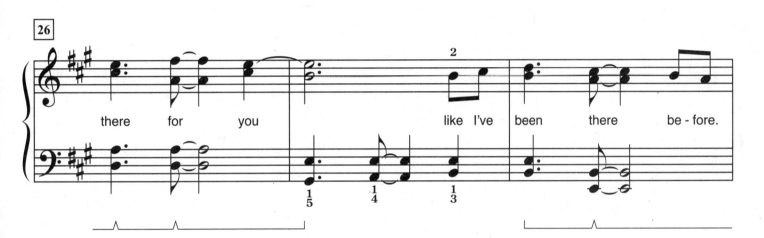

there for you like I've been there be-fore.

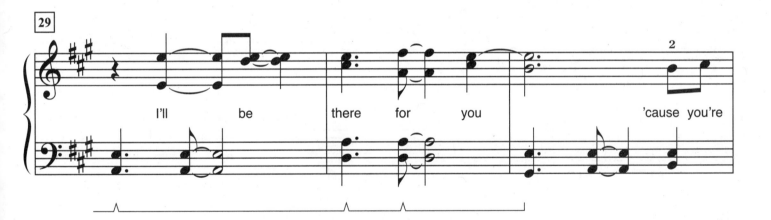

I'll be there for you 'cause you're

there for me, too. *rit.* *mf*

Use after pages 60–61.

Shallow
(from *A Star Is Born*)

Words and Music by Lady Gaga, Mark Ronson,
Anthony Rossomando and Andrew Wyatt
Arr. by Tom Gerou

Moderate folk rock

Tell me some-thin', girl,   are you hap-py in this
Tell me some-thing, boy,   aren't you tired tryin' to

mod-ern world,   or do you need more?
fill that void,   or do you need more?

Is there some-thin' else you're search-in' for?
Ain't it hard keep-in' it so hard - core?
I'm fall -

in'. In all the good times, I find my-self long-in'

for change. And in the bad times, I

fear my-self. I'm off the deep end, watch as I dive in.